WHY I SERGEANT STUBBY GO TO WAR?

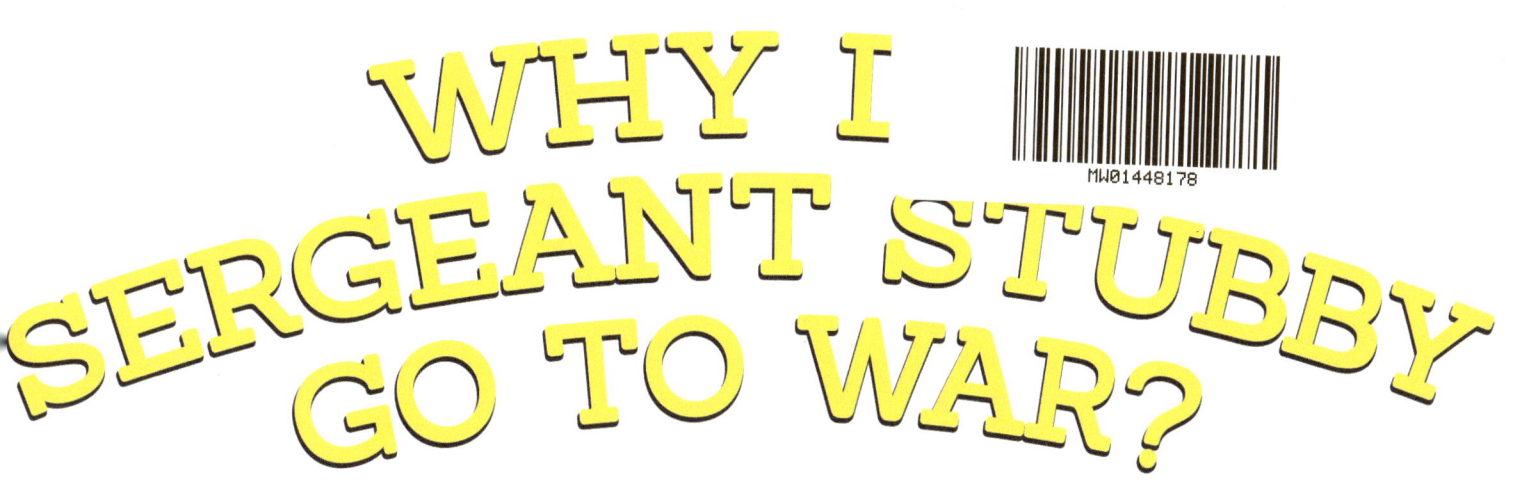

WRITTEN BY:
CATHY WERLING

ILLUSTRATED BY:
CHRISTINA GARCIA

PUBLISHED BY:

Lowell Milken Center
FOR *Unsung Heroes*
Discover Create Change

© 2018 LOWELL MILKEN CENTER FOR UNSUNG HEROES
ALL RIGHTS RESERVED

You, too, have a special hero hiding inside —
Cathy Werling

Frankie just couldn't wait! Papa Conroy had come for a visit, and dinner was finally over. Now it was Frankie's favorite part of the day. During Papa's visits, evening time also meant story time. Frankie thought Papa told the most fascinating stories, and he was very anxious to hear about another of his grandpa's adventures.

As Papa walked into the living room and sat in the big easy chair, Frankie hurried to sit at his feet. Wide-eyed and wiggling with anticipation, he said, "Papa Conroy, will you please tell me a story?"

"Of course, Frankie," said Papa. "I have the perfect story tonight. It's about a dog who was very special to me . . . and became very special to many others, too. He was what I call an "unsung hero," someone who helped others in an important way, but not many people know about it."

"Oh, I have to hear this," said Frankie's older brother, Carl, as he entered the room. Frankie motioned for Carl to come and sit beside him on the floor as Papa began his story . . .

"It started back in 1917 when I was training with other soldiers during World War I. We were doing our training drills on the campus of Yale University when a little brown and white dog wandered onto the grounds."

"He just hung around us, not wanting to leave. He seemed so lonely and very hungry. I just knew he needed me. So I took him in and cared for him."

"That small dog captured our hearts and soon became part of our troop. With his little bit of a tail and his short legs, we just knew that 'Stubby' would be the perfect name for him."

"When I wasn't busy with my training duties, I was spending a lot of time with Stubby. He was such a smart dog and learned tricks very easily. Once he learned how to shake hands, I taught him to reach higher and higher. It wasn't long before Stubby was reaching high enough to enable him to learn how to salute!"

"Stubby had become one of us, a member of our troop. Once our training was done, I could not bear the thought of leaving him behind when we boarded the transport ship that would take us across the ocean to begin our war duties."

"Dogs, of course, were forbidden on the ship, so I had to sneak him on board and hide him in the coal bin on the lower level. The ship set sail, and all went well until one day our commanding officer saw that Stubby was on board!"

"The time had come! I quickly gave Stubby the signal, and he saluted the officer. I thought our commander was going to fall over from laughing. He instantly loved Stubby just as much as the rest of us did, and Stubby became a part of our troop! He was given special orders allowing him to accompany our division to the front lines as our mascot. He even had his own set of dog tags."

"We had a scare one day, however, when Stubby became very ill. He was used to the loud sounds of war, but in this case, he had become very sick from exposure to a dangerous gas used by the enemy. Stubby was taken to a hospital and nursed back to health. I remember being so worried, not realizing that something good would come from this scary situation."

"Because of his sickness from the gas, Stubby could detect its presence, even though it had no smell or color. Gas attacks usually happened early in the morning when most of us were asleep. Stubby immediately knew when gas was in the air and ran through the trenches, barking and biting at our shirts to get our attention. Someone would then sound the gas alarm so that we could put on the gas masks that would save us from breathing in the dangerous gas."

"Stubby's sense of hearing also became very important to all of us. He was trained to whine when he heard incoming artillery shells, which alerted all of us to take cover before our human ears could even pick up the sound. I shudder to think what could have happened to us without that early warning."

"One night Stubby heard an enemy spy sneaking into the camp. The spy spotted Stubby and tried to quietly get the dog to come to him. However, Stubby started barking, and when the spy tried to run, Stubby used his teeth to grab the spy's leg so that he could not escape. By then, some of us heard the noise and came to help capture the enemy. Once again, Stubby had saved the day! Because of this brave act, our commanding officer promoted Stubby to the rank of Sergeant."

"Along with capturing that enemy spy, Stubby was so important in the rescue of many of our wounded soldiers. He was able to tell the difference between the soldiers who spoke our language and those who spoke the language of the enemy. He could then direct us to where we needed to go to rescue our soldiers. Many soldiers were saved because of Stubby's bravery."

"By the end of the war, I considered Stubby to be my best friend. We had gone through 17 battles together. When we returned to our country, Stubby got to meet many important people, even the president of the United States! He also received medals for everything that he had done."

"That next fall, I entered law school at Georgetown University. Stubby went with me and became the mascot of the Georgetown Hoyas. He even provided entertainment by pushing a football across the football field at halftime. He was a dog of many talents!"

Frankie and Carl were in awe as their grandfather finished his story. They couldn't believe that a little dog was capable of so much, especially such great acts of heroism.

As Papa Conroy reached in his pocket, he asked the boys if they would like to see a picture of Stubby. "Yes!" both children stated in unison, eager to see the amazing little dog.

As he lovingly looked at the photo before showing it to the boys, it was easy to see how much Stubby still meant to Papa. "Do you miss him?" Frankie asked.

"Oh, every day! Stubby may be gone, but he will live in my heart forever. What that little guy taught me is something that many people in this world have never learned. He taught me to value each life and to see the worth of every individual."

"I often think how different things would have been if we had shooed that little scraggly, homeless dog away when he wandered into our training area. How many lives would have been lost or left untouched without him?"

HERO

"'Papa, people could be like that, too, couldn't they?' Frankie thought aloud, his voice trailing off, as his mind wandered to that lonely, dirty-looking little boy he'd seen at the park that morning, and finally . . . to himself. Was it possible that each of them also had a hero hiding inside, just like Stubby?"

Other Interesting Facts

- During World War I, it was Private J. Robert Conroy of the 102nd Infantry, 26th Yankee Division, who found and named Stubby. When the division shipped out for France aboard the SS Minnesota, Stubby was aboard. He was also with the 102nd Infantry when they reached the front lines in February of 1918.

- After capturing a German enemy spy, Stubby received a promotion to the rank of Sergeant by the commander of the 102nd Infantry. He became the first dog to be given rank in the United States Armed Forces. He then outranked Conroy, who was, by then, a Corporal!

- Later, after his hospitalization from the gas attack, Stubby was injured during a grenade attack, receiving a large amount of shrapnel in his chest and leg. He was rushed to a field hospital and later transferred to a Red Cross Recovery Hospital for additional surgery. When Stubby became well enough to move around at the hospital, he visited wounded soldiers, boosting their spirits.

- During the war, Stubby participated in 17 battles and four major campaigns. He earned one Wound Chevron (predecessor to the Purple Heart) and three Overseas Service Chevrons for his time in battle.

- After the war ended, Conroy brought Stubby back to the United States with him where Stubby was treated as a national hero. Stubby toured the country doing promotions to sell war bonds. He was given awards, took part in parades, and even met with three separate sitting U.S. Presidents (Woodrow Wilson, Warren Harding and Calvin Coolidge). Stubby was awarded many medals for his heroism, including a medal from the Humane Society which was presented by General John Pershing, the Commanding General of the United States Armies.

- In early 1926, Stubby's health began to fail, and on March 16th of that year, the tiny WWI veteran passed away in the loving arms of his friend and comrade, J. Robert Conroy.

- Today, Stubby's remains are on display as part of the Smithsonian exhibit, *The Price of Freedom: Americans at War*, in Washington, D.C. Stubby was also honored on November 11, 2006, with a brick in the Walk of Honor at the National World War I Museum at the *Liberty Memorial* in Kansas City, Missouri.

CPSIA information can be obtained
at www.ICGtesting.com
Printed in the USA
LVHW070341241221
707090LV00002B/13